this is how i knew.

by
kiana azizian

kiana azizian

my love.

i'm sorry we couldn't
make this work.

perhaps,
one day we will find
our way back to one another.

i'll be missing you.

i wasn't sure i'd ever
find the strength to leave.
until one morning,
it all hit me.
hard.
it knocked the wind
from my lungs,
and brought me
to my knees.
i was breathless,
helpless.
hopeless.
i knew what
needed to be done,
there was no other way.

so i caught my breath,
picked myself up.
then pull myself together,
and did the inevitable.
i left.

and in the process,
i set myself free.

i am so regretful of the fact
i could not love you the
way you deserved.

- the apology you never received

i am sorry for all
the promises i broke.
i am sorry for all the things
i said that turned into lies.

i am so sorry
for all of this.

- oh how i am sorry

oh heartbreak,
how we never see it coming,
and are never ready for the
colossal effect it has on our lives.

but what happens when
we are the one breaking hearts.
when we are the
one who pulls the trigger.
does it hurt any less?
does our heart break
in a different way,
in a different place?

we've all been told
how to heal from heartbreak,
how to grieve and carry on.
how to rebuild then move on.

we are never
prepared for the
destroying.
the wrecking.
we are never told
what to do when we
are the ones who are
not only hurting,
but also have to live with
blood on our hands.

our fire burned out.

and we've been living
in the dark ever since.

i broke myself in hopes
you would find parts
of me to love.
pieces of me that you
would appeal to your
taste buds.
the more you
pushed me away,
the harder i shattered.
the further you threw me,
the harder i tried to be
the one who you
could love forever.

give all your sorrows
to the ocean.

the waves can take
them from here,
my dear.

inevitability,
i am drowning in
your shallow affection.

- danger ahead

i love myself too much
to settle for your
depthless love.

- shallow love

i waited so long for love.
years to be exact.
i yearned for it
craved it.
would crumble
even at the thought of it.
one day,
i got what i always wanted.
sweet sweet love.
the easy kind of love.
the kind kind of love.
the kind of love even
love would be jealous of.

then one morning,
i woke up,
with that forgotten longing,
that initial thirst.
nostalgic for a love
that once was mine.
and just like that,
i realized my love was gone.

it was no longer mine,
no longer yours.

it was no longer
ours.

what is love if
you do not fall,
do not drown,
deeply,
immensely,
fully into it?

maybe for now,
we can settle on
becoming lost lovers.

- until then, i'll be missing you

be brave
and stand up
for what you believe in.

the world won't dare
stand in your way.

perhaps it's better
to have bullet wounds in
the chest than to be the
one standing behind the gun.

- *perspective*

hurting you was
never in my intentions.
i regret how you got
caught in the crossfire of
my self-discovery.

- *i guess i have bad aim*

even after all this time,
i still feel your ocean,
raging away,
recklessly,
inside of me.

to be honest,
i was afraid of
being single again.
being on my own,
alone.
i was scared
of the unknown,
the uncertainty
and instability.

i convinced myself
it was better
to be with someone
then to be on my own.

i was wrong.
staying in a loveless
relationship was hard.
but i think what
was even worst,
was losing myself,
at the false hope
of fleeting love.

i wanted love so badly,
i shoved you in a
place you didn't fit.
smothering myself
in the process
of trying to love you.
suffocating,
at the thought
of being yours.

it breaks my heart to think
so many of you are stuck
in loveless relationships.

it breaks my heart to think
so many of you are
too scared to leave,
crippled by fear.

it breaks my heart to think
you lie awake at night,
breathless,
holding back tears,
instead of sleeping.

it breaks my heart to think
you've quit.
you've given up.
you've settled.

it breaks my heart to think
you've convinced yourself
this is what you deserve,
desire.

it breaks my heart to know
so many of you are heartbroken,
living in broken homes,
with broken hearts.

love doesn't feel like this,
shouldn't feel like this.

love shouldn't be this hard,
this difficult,
this exhausting,
this draining.

love isn't meant to tear us apart,
tear us down,
mess us up.

love didn't set out to destroy us,
wreck us,
ruin us.

- love should be healing, always

i have detached
so far from myself,
i am hardly here
anymore.

- i have become a ghost trying to love you

it was crazy how
easily i fell back
into my old self.

it was like i was
searching around,
quietly sitting,
waiting,
for myself,
all along.

- long overdue

out of fear,
i was too stubborn
to let you go.

the battle between
my head and my heart
is getting too loud.

how can one person
be torn in such
different directions?

who am i now that i've gone?

what have we done?

where do i go from here?

when will this pain disappear?

why did we have to end up like this?

- the five Ws

this is how i knew

destroying you destroyed me.

- repercussions

i'm not sure i'll ever
recover from destroying you.

- a harsh truth i will live with forever

i walked away.
not because you didn't
want me to stay,
but because i needed
to free myself.

these scars do not define you,
let them carry you to the heavens.

- wings

the world stopped
turning when i left.
even gravity didn't
know what to do.

- *we all lost ourselves that day*

the day i left,
i could feel
my own heart
shattering from
one to a million.

- *i cannot imagine what happened to yours*

i thought things
would get better.
with time.
with age.
with circumstance.
no.
no.
no.
none of it was enough.
i waited and waited
and i waited.
seasons changed,
but everything
remained the same.
days turned to months,
then those months
turn into years.
time was slipping away.
time was moving forward.
evolving.
but we got left behind.
stuck in our ways.
struggling to be the
people who we once were.
my patience had run low.
i couldn't stand back
and wait any longer.
i couldn't take this
loveless love anymore.

... but you never asked me to stay.

how did we end up so alone?
i asked the man on the moon.

because we were willing to
fight for what we deserve,
he reminded me.

we all have a little wild,
a little madness,
a little chaos
within us.

i am caught in this war
of wanting to love you,
but needing to leave you.

- a want verse a need

loving you was
a beautiful irony.

leaving you was
a beautiful tragedy.

- ironic tragedy

and even after i'm gone,
look in your heart.
i'll always be there.

- i promise

will you be my safety?

or

will you be my storm?

will you be my shelter?

or

will you be my destruction?

what are the lies you
tell yourself late at night?

what are the things
that won't let you go to sleep?

why does the darkness
have so much power over you?

- *late night conversations*

listen to your gut.
she always knows best.

she will tell you all the
things you already know.
all the things you are
too scared to hear,
all the things you are
too stubborn to accept.

i knew what needed
to be done.

i was just scared of
hurting you in the process
of liberating myself.

there is nothing romantic
about leaving a lover.
it is painful.
heart-breaking,
literally.
it is dreadful.
terrible.
no,
there is nothing
romantic about this act.
sometimes,
it is just simply necessary.
sometimes,
it is the only thing that
can be done,
in order to
survive.

this blame,
and this remorse,
they will not leave.
will not disappear.
they cling,
claw,
tear into me.
ripping apart what little is
left of my heart.
what little is left of me.
then the heartache came along,
reminding me of everything i lost.
everything that's been
taken away from me.
the sorrow stole my breath.
my lungs collapsed
under all the pressure.
i forgot how to breathe.
i was convinced i
wouldn't survive this.
this was the end.
then out of nowhere,
mercy came.
it was gentle and kind.
calming.
understanding.
it brought me to my knees,
and gave me a second chance
at this thing called life.

it is better to be alone,
than to be with
someone who drains the
life from your veins.

- know your worth

i'm not really sure who
i'll be without you.
but i hope i will
be better than this.

- faith in fate

this is me,
learning,
how to let
go of you.

this is me,
learning,
how to love
myself,
once again.

- the cure

remember what it took
for you to bloom.
don't be too quick to
pick your own flowers.

- self-destruction

be strong enough
to leave a relationship
that does not make
you the best
version of yourself.

be brave enough
to give your heart
what it asks for.

walking away from you,
finally set me free from
myself.

i am tired
of breaking myself,
in order to make you whole.
giving and giving,
only for you to take and take.
i am tired of waiting,
for things to get better,
for everything to go back
to the way they used to be.
i am tired of waiting
for change,
for redemption.

one day,
when i'm ready,
i will walk away.
i will give all my
love to myself.
the very same love you
took for granted.
i will give and give to myself,
until i am whole again.

and i hope someday,
you will realize the type
of love i gave to you.
how much i gave to you.
and how you were never
really worthy of any of it.

do you remember the flame
of the fire you used to
carry around with you?

do you remember what
it felt like to burn?

do you remember what
it felt like to feel alive?

our love story got lost to the waves.

- crash and drown

i think even love was rooting for us.

- and it still wasn't enough

my heart.
my instinct.
my intuition.
my gut.

they all knew before i did.

keep moving forward.

no matter what
you left in the past.

no matter who
you left behind.

sometimes,
it is necessary
to be a little selfish.

it's okay to put
yourself first,
sometimes.

do you miss me,
when the sun drops
to its knees,
when the man on the
moon goes to sleep?

do you miss me,
when you're alone,
in the dark of the night,
when you're wrapped
in the cold of your sheets?

do you miss me,
when you wake up alone,
with a void in your bed,
and an even bigger
void in your heart?

do you ever miss me,
like i miss you?

i knew in my heart
what needed
to be done.

i just couldn't find
the strength in my
bones to leave.

we were crazy in love.

now,
this love is driving
us crazy.

i have made my bed.

and now,
i will lay here,
until it doesn't
hurt so much,
to breathe.

i tried so hard to
be your life raft,
i didn't notice i was
drowning myself in
the process of trying
to save you.

the more i tried
to make you
fall back in
love with me,
the less i valued
my own self.

you know
what you deserve.

take the risk,
and go for it.

because regret
never seems to
really fade.

i write to help you heal.

i write to help you
understand
that it gets better.
it always does get better.

i write to remind you
there is still hope.
there is still faith.
fate.

i write to help you
feel a little less
on your own,
to remind you that
you are never alone,
and you never will be.
(because you always have me.)

i write to let you
know that no matter
how broken you are,
how shattered you feel.

there is always healing.
there is always help.
there is always hope.

allow your pain to remind
you how powerful you were,
and how powerful you still are.

allow your hurt to show you
how far you have come,
and how far you are
still able to go.

do not feel guilty
for putting yourself first.
there is no shame in doing
what is best for you.
there is no shame in fighting
for your own happiness,
for fighting for yourself.

- in case you have forgotten

some nights,
i still dream about you.
about us.
and the way we used to be.
i dream about how you
used to tilt your head back
as you laughed at me,
and how the sound of your laugh
would make me laugh.
i dream about your touch,
and the control it
used to have over me.
how my body would
fall to pieces with
just one stroke.
just one kiss.
i dream about meeting
you again one day.
about how you would look
at me in a way you haven't in years,
and how it would make me question
why i ever decided to leave.
i dream about us finding
our way back to each other.
how maybe we would
be able to make it work.
how if gotten the chance,
we would be better off
the second time around.

you will always have
a piece of my broken,
tattered,
confused,
and messy heart.

take this moment,
this opportunity,
this breath,
to transform into
the person who you
always desired to be.
rediscover who you are.
who you were before them,
who you want to be,
now,
that they are gone.

- good things can come from endings to

this is how i knew

there is nothing beautiful
about walking away.

it is the ugliest thing
i've ever done.

- i will not glorify my actions

i never wanted to carry
this label upon my soul.
i never wanted this to be
a part of my title.

- heartbreaker

i am still learning
how to be
selfish and selfless,
simultaneously,
together,
and all at once.

- *the art of balance*

we stay together,
destroying each other,
because we're afraid
our worlds will
be destroyed,
if we do not stay together.

all of a sudden,
you've found yourself lost.
confused,
and forgotten.
misplaced.
pain has overtaken you,
replacing all the love.
replacing all the softness.

you are tired,
weary.
but worst of all drained.
you poured so much of
yourself into someone else.
a person who
didn't appreciate
how much of yourself
you give them.
how much of yourself
you lost to them.
how much you loved them.

the truth is,
you will never get those
parts of yourself back.
they are gone,
lost forever.
you will never be that
same person again...

but this,
is where the magic lives.

now you have the opportunity
to become a better person.
to become the real you.
you have the chance
to become the person
who you were
always meant to be.

appreciation this time,
take advantage of it to the fullest
(you may never get it again).

find yourself,
and recreate yourself anew.
grow into you.

because that is something
they will never be able
to take away from you.

it gets exhausting relying
on others for your happiness.

maybe it's time to find
some on your own,
for yourself.

i broke.
completely shattered.
crashed.
scattered across the floor.

day by day,
i picked myself up.

and day by day,
i glued pieces of
myself back together.

i am whole again.

different,
yet somehow still the same.

falling in love with you,
only to leave you,
was by far,
one of the hardest
things i've ever had,
and will ever have,
to do.

- *fleeting love*

love her right,
or she'll walk away.

- *simple as that*

my mind
carries my heart.
it often seems
to know best.
but every so often,
my mind quiets
and lets my heart
take control.

this,
is when the
magic begins.

what if i'm making a mistake?

what if i never find anyone else?

what if i end up lonely,
forgotten,
and alone?

what if i just let go of the
best thing i'll ever have?

what if i spend the rest of my
life wondering *what if?*

- *doubts*

you are beautiful,
a goddess.
true incredible.
but somewhere along the way
you've convinced yourself
that you are broken,
and can never be fixed.
the darkness and the pain,
they have become a part of you.
you let them in and entertain them,
make them a cup of tea.
holding on to them,
in hopes that they will make
you feel a little less alone.
you pick at your scars,
never really giving them
the time they need to heal,
to fade.
you are convinced that
you need to stay strong,
and never show anyone
that you are in pain,
in so much hurt.
there is no need to
bear this on your own.
you are so loved and never alone.
you are incredible.
a goddess.
truly beautiful.

in-between these pages,
this is where our story
will continue to breathe.

maybe here is where
our love will carry on
and live.

you've hidden your heart.
from the world,
from yourself.
you've locked it up,
built a wall,
put up barriers.
you think you are fighting,
protecting yourself.
you are doing what's right.

but my darling,
no good ever comes
from hiding your heart.

you are greater than this.
you are stronger than this.

take down those walls,
smash that cement.
breakthrough,
break open.
let your heart out,
and let the world see the real you.

your heart deserves
to be happy and free.
your heart deserves
to be loved,
it deserves to be cherished.

how did you know?
they ask.

how could i not?
i reply.

i'll be waiting for you
in our next lifetime.

perhaps,
then,
we will get this
whole thing right.

i think i've forgotten
what it feels like
to be happy.
what it feels like
to be at peace,
(and not in pieces).

somewhere,
along the way,
i lost all the best
parts of myself.
pieces that were
never yours to take.

but you did anyway.

there's a massive
difference between
being content
and truly happy.

- i'm sure you already know where you stand

finally,
for the first time
in months i feel like
the person i used to be.

- the healing always comes

there is a real danger
in making yourself
invisible.
unseen.
unnoticeable.
silencing your voice.
quietly tiptoeing around.
slowly thinning,
disappearing.

until one day,
there is none of you left.
nothing but a faded
version of yourself.
of who you used to be.

true love should
not be suffocating.
belittling.
it should not be
damaging.

love should
encourage you.
inspire you.
it should help
you reach the fullest
of your potential.

i can't help but think:

perhaps,
we were just using
each other
to pass those
lonely nights.

perhaps,
we just need
someone.

we just need,
someone,
anyone.

you used to look
at me with a hunger
in your eyes.
a thirst.
a longing,
that was just for me.

you used to make me
feel beautiful.
like a goddess.

but now,
you look straight
through me.
like i'm not even
here anymore.

the eyes i fell for
now make me feel
i n v i s i b l e.

i don't know
how to love you,
without losing
myself.

because losing myself
to you,
to love,
would completely
destroy me.

we settle for misery,
because we are so
afraid of change.
scared our lives
will end up in ruins.
our lives will end
up in nothing.

so,
we accept
how things are,
convince ourselves
they will never
get better,
and believe that things
will never change.

for once,
i am not running away.

i am standing up for
what i deserve.

i am fighting for something
bigger than myself.

i miss the
beginning days.
where this was all so new.
when we were
still intrigued,
captivated,
with each other.
when we were enchanted
by the idea of love.

but somewhere along
our journey,
we forgot how to love
one another.
how to love ourselves.
we forgot the magic of
the beginning days,
the simplicity of
the good old days.

and we let the world get
the best of us.

first came guilt,
then came the shame.
followed by my
oldest friend sadness.

over time,
acceptance came to me
and asked for forgiveness.

together,
they all lead me to freedom.

- the stages of moving on

i hope you find your peace
in someone else.
and i hope your
new life is stunning.

i hope you find everything
your heart is looking for.

i hope one day,
we will get together
and look back on
the good times.

i hope one day,
we can undo this mess.

i hope one day,
we wouldn't have to be
strangers anymore,
and this won't all
hurt so much.

i hope one day,
you can forgive me,
so i can forgive myself.

- i'll be rooting for you

let's admit it:
both our hearts
went cold.
both of us stopped
putting in the effort.
both of us are
to blame for all this.

i cannot keep hoping,
praying,
waiting
for us to fall back in love
with one another.

you make excuses,
for them,
for yourself.
saying that you cannot leave,
it's too late.
it's never too late.
it's too hard.
and so is staying.
people will get hurt.
you are hurting.
you cannot survive without them.
you already are.
you cannot be without them.
they aren't even there anymore.

so you stay.
you do anything to
quiet that voice,
that reasoning.
you know it's all wrong,
and you know what
can make it right.

all you need is a little courage
and a lot of strength.
you can do this,
i believe in you.

nold on to your heart
until you find the person
who brings you back to life.
the one who rekindles your fire,
and keeps you aflame.
hold on to your heart
until you find the person
who is worth skipping beats for.

i have been hurt,
and i have hurt others.

i have been left,
and in the end,
i have been
the one to leave.

i have been forgotten
by people i loved,
and i have forgotten
my loved ones.

i have loved,
and i have lost
that very same love.

- what goes around, comes around

we do not grow
when we are
standing still.

we do not bloom
when we are holding
on to the past.

- remaining stagnant is deadly

people change.
people grow apart.

and sometimes,
people fade away.

- including us

not everyone will
feel like home.

not everyone is
worth unpacking for.

not everyone is
going to hold
your heart gently
in their hands.

i tried lying to myself.
telling myself it will get better.
it would pass.
this was a phase,
just a chapter in our lives.
we were just stuck in a funk,
(a long funk).
but time didn't prove differently,
things stayed the same.
they never changed.

honestly,
i knew deep down the solution.
but honestly,
i was too scared to listen.
too scared to accept the
truth staring right at me,
with pity dripping from its eyes.

so i did what i could,
doing anything to quiet
that little voice.
telling her she was wrong.
this cannot be true.
she didn't know what she
was talking about.
this is how things are supposed to be.
i silenced her.
i shut her up...

and in the process,
i silenced myself.
this is for the better.
i kept telling her.
this is what is right.
i kept reminding myself.

but,
neither of us were convinced.
we both knew the truth.
how can this be true?
i was scared,
absolutely terrified.
horrified.
but the longer i stayed,
the less of me remained.
the longer i stayed,
the more of me vanished.

one morning,
i pulled together the courage,
and did what needed to be done.
i cut ties and in the process,
found the independence
i had been gasping for.
i found my freedom.
i was finally,
completely,
liberated.

some nights,
i lay awake,
next to you,
wondering what
it would be like
to fall asleep in
my own arms.

- i'm lonely even though i'm not alone

me,
in your arms,
was the safest
place in the world.

- nostalgia

it wasn't all bad.
i still remember the
sound of your laugh,
the curve of your smile.
how we used to stay
up late at night
telling each other
our dreams,
our fears.
days spent in bed,
nights spent under the stars,
hours spent wrapped up
in each other's arms.

oh,
how easy it was
for us to fall in
(and out)
of love.

there is no beauty in
this type of brokenness.

it lives in the redemption.

- it lives in the rebirth

i replay it all,
trying to pinpoint the
exact moment we
got this wrong.
trying to understand
how we fell apart.

and no matter how
many times,
i watch the story of us,
i can never figure
out how we drifted
so far away from ourselves.

what a shame that you are
so scared of being
on your own,
that you stay in an
unhealthy relationship.
a relationship that is
draining the life
from your eyes.
the softness
from your skin.

you feel alone.
lonely,
even though you have
someone sitting right
there next to you.

how is that okay?
how is that love?

how did you even get here?

you are in love with
someone who is incapable
of giving you the type
of love you need.
the type of love you
thought you had,
but now realize
it was all a lie...

why are you holding on,
clinging,
to a love that does
not exist anymore?
a love that is lost,
and cannot be found again.

why are you staying
in a relationship you
promised you never would.

in time,
you will find your power
and your courage.
your resilience.
and you will be brave enough
to do what's best for you.

in time,
you will value yourself
enough to fight for you,
 and to put yourself first.

in time,
you will find the strength
to walk away.
to walk toward
what you truly deserve.

walking away does
not make you weak.

it takes strength to
stand up for what your
heart knows is true.

it takes courage to
leave.

it takes courage to
be brave.

i wonder if you got
tired of hearing it as
much as i did saying it.

- i'm fine.

they keep telling
me to be strong,
but i've given all
my strength away.

- defeat

the day we stopped
arguing was the same
day we stopped fighting
for each other.

it's time to start
saving yourself.
to start putting time and
energy into the
things you want,
the things you need.
it's time to start fighting,
for yourself,
for your heart.

because at the end of the day,
you are the only one who
can change your world.
the only person who
can change your soul.
take control,
do what needs to be done.
it's time.
it's time.

it's time.

find your truth.
write it on the walls.
scream it from your lungs.
bring it to life.
make it your existence.

- make it your reality

it's okay to be tired,
to be exhausted.

it's okay to not
be so strong,
so brave all the time.

- it's okay to not be okay

this is how i knew

there's a fire in
your gentleness you
must never let go out.

i guess if i really,
truly loved you,
i wouldn't have left.

i guess if you truly,
really loved me,
you would have asked
me to stay.

i guess if we truly really
love one another,
we would have never
gotten in this mess.

i used to love how
we never augured.

but now,
i wished we'd disagree,
scream,
yell,
shout.

at least this way,
we'd be feeling
something.

we'd be fighting
for one another.
we'd have something
worth fighting for.

- passion

i thought i'd be
devastated now that
you aren't around.
i'd be lost
without you.

and yes,
it was hard.
the hardest thing
i've ever done-
especially in
the beginning.

but my world didn't
come crashing down.
the sky didn't fall,
the ocean didn't
drown itself.
the sun still shined.
the sky cleared up,
while the rain washed
everything away.

i doubted myself for so long.
belittling myself into nothing.
questioning my strength,
my drive.
my ambition
my worth...

there was a time
where i truly believed
i wouldn't come out of this alive,
that i wouldn't ever recover
from you,
from any of this.

but over time,
i realized that i was
better off without you.
i was fine on my own,
great on my own.
i did it.

i survived this.

i survived you.

it may be hard
for you to believe.

but despite it all,

i still love you.

- and i think i always will

our time together
was not wasted.
i will never forget
the love we shared.
the love that gave us hope.
i will never forget the
strength you,
and your love
taught me.

it's true what they say:

women like me
never stay.

women like me
should never try
to be tamed.

women like me
destroy
people like you.

when you look up at the sky,
i hope you search for me
between the stars.

- *i'll always be there*

you are so fearful
of the unknown,
you're suffocating
in the familiarity
of comfort.

- break free

i always thought
falling out of love
took time.
days,
months,
even years.

but for me,
it wasn't like that.
it didn't take much time.

it was sudden.
overnight.

one evening
i was falling asleep to
the sound of your
beating heart,
only to wake up
wondering what
happened to mine.

- *change of heart*

before i knew it,
i had changed
myself for you.

i toned myself down,
turned myself off.
i kept my mouth shut.

i closed my door,
changed the locks,
blocked out all my windows,
built my walls back up.

i thought that if there
was less of me around,
i'd be easier to love.

this is not how a
relationship should be.

this is not how we
should have loved
one another.

you've got the moon on your side,
nothing is impossible.

- go after what you deserve

                              the only thing
                        harder than leaving,
                          would be staying.

                        - lose-lose situation

i never thought
this love
- our love -
would have an
expiration date.

i never thought
our love
would have fled
so easily.

- i honestly thought we would last forever

just because our
love had an end,
does not mean,
our story will
be forgotten.

perhaps one day,
when we're older,
we'll run into each other,
and laugh about this all.

perhaps that day,
you will thank me
for leaving
and i can finally
forgive myself.

perhaps one day,
you will look at me
with that look
in your eye,
and i will remember
what it felt like to be
loved by you.

perhaps on that day,
we will remember
the good times,
remember all the
good memories
we shared.
and at that moment,
this all won't hurt
as much...

perhaps one day,
you and i can be more
than just two people
who used to be in love.

perhaps one day,
we,
will be okay.

perhaps,
we will be,
more than okay.

perhaps,
we will be
better than
just okay.

perhaps..

kiana azizian

thank you for your light.
thank you for your love.
thank you for helping me find my way.

until next time.
xx

Made in the USA
San Bernardino, CA
01 May 2020